Original title:
Craters of Comedy

Copyright © 2025 Creative Arts Management OÜ
All rights reserved.

Author: Liam Sterling
ISBN HARDBACK: 978-1-80567-872-4
ISBN PAPERBACK: 978-1-80567-993-6

Jovial Impact

In a world where chuckles bloom,
Laughter echoes, fills the room.
Jesters dance on moonlit beams,
Tickling fate with lively dreams.

Bubbles burst with joyful cheers,
Silly sounds delight our ears.
The cosmos sways, a playful tune,
Where giggles float like stars in June.

Whimsical Shadows

In shadows deep, a giggle hides,
Where fickle whimsy dances wide.
A twist of fate, a wink of chance,
Invites you to a jolly dance.

Lopsided hats and shoes so bright,
Prance around with pure delight.
Each chuckle forms a playful path,
Leading us to joyous wrath.

Celestial Grooves

Stars conspire in a cosmic jest,
As comets twirl, they become the best.
Planets spin with a carefree grace,
Filling space with a merry face.

Asteroids bounce with cheeky flair,
Creating laughter in the air.
Galaxies swirl with a rhythmic sway,
Fueling fun in a zany way.

Galactic Giggles

In the deep of night, a chuckle roams,
Tickling planets in their homes.
Laughter travels through the void,
Bringing joy no one can avoid.

Silly aliens play their part,
Crafting smiles with cosmic art.
With every quirk and every sound,
A universe of fun is found.

Laughter in Low Gravity

In a world where giggles fly,
Bouncing jokes up to the sky.
Rubber chickens float around,
Laughs and snorts are truly found.

Upside-down, we take a dive,
With each pun, we feel alive.
Gravity can't pull us down,
In this wacky, joyful town.

Impactful Humor

A joke lands like a meteor,
Crashing in with such rapport.
Spilling laughs like cosmic dust,
In giggles and guffaws, we trust.

Each punchline hits, a joyful boom,
Filling up the laughter room.
With every quip, we soar and sway,
Count the chuckles, night and day.

Harmonies of Hilarity

Melodies of laughter ring,
Silly songs that make us sing.
Witty lines dance in the air,
A chorus of joy everywhere.

Boisterous notes create a tide,
In giggles, all our fears subside.
In this symphony of jest,
Find the humor that's the best.

Cosmic Capers

Adventures in the cosmic void,
Where laughter is the best decoy.
Space clowns juggling stars so bright,
Turn mistakes into delight.

Across the galaxies we roam,
With every laugh, we find a home.
In the chaos, joy prevails,
Riding on these comic trails.

The Jester's Crater

In the valley where jests collide,
Laughter echoes, nowhere to hide.
Bright colors swirl, like pies in flight,
Clowns parade beneath the spotlight.

Big shoes bounce on the moon's soft face,
Gravity's pull can't slow down the pace.
With every pratfall, joy finds room,
In a wacky world where chuckles zoom.

Comedic Perspectives in Space

Stars giggle as they twinkle bright,
While asteroids roll in their cosmic plight.
Silly aliens share goofy tales,
Zooming past in their rubbery sails.

Planets wink with a playful spin,
Orbiting jokes, let the fun begin.
In the vastness, where humor ignites,
Space is ripe for whimsical flights.

Quirkiness in the Void

In emptiness where oddities sing,
Balloons drift by on a celestial fling.
Floating fish in a jellybean sea,
Guffaws ripple, wild and free.

With hiccups of stardust in the air,
Quirky giggles bubble everywhere.
The universe spins, a jest so grand,
In this madcap, whimsical land.

Laughing with Lunars

Moonbeams dance with a giggling grace,
Spinning tales in a celestial space.
Frogs on rocks croak a comic rhyme,
Tickling stars, oh, what a time!

With every bounce of a lunar hop,
Laughter rings, it never will stop.
In a land where even shadows play,
The joy of jest lights up the way.

Comedic Cosmos

In a galaxy filled with jest,
Stars giggle and puff their chest.
Planets spinning in a dance,
While asteroids join in the prance.

Laughter echoes through the skies,
Comets chuckle as they fly.
Space dust tickles the moon's face,
In this cosmic, silly space.

Radiant Ridicule

A sunbeam grins, a vibrant hue,
Tickling clouds as they drift through.
Rainbows tease with colors bright,
In every shade, a playful sight.

Stars poke fun at the night sky,
Winking softly, oh so sly.
Bright meteors launch one-liners,
In the void, they're the great shiners.

Stellar Smiles

Bubbles of laughter burst like stars,
Light-years away, yet never far.
Jokes orbit near the brightest sun,
As twilight joins in the fun.

Satellites spin with glee and cheer,
Echoing giggles, loud and clear.
With each twist, the cosmos beams,
A universe built on whims and dreams.

The Lighthearted Chasm

In a canyon deep, laughter bounces,
Echoes of joy prompt us to pounce.
Silly shadows stretch and play,
Dancing wildly throughout the day.

Ledges grin with whimsical hair,
While rocks roll over without care.
In this chasm where chuckles reign,
A tapestry of humor gains.

Craters of Joy

In a world where giggles bloom,
Laughter dances, fills the room.
Silly faces, jolly pranks,
Joy is found in playful ranks.

Bouncing hops and clumsy falls,
Every slip, a chorus calls.
Bright balloons and sticky treats,
Life's a stage with funny feats.

Laughing Landscapes

Hills that chuckle, valleys grin,
Every hilltop holds a whim.
Clouds that tickle, winds that tease,
Nature joins in joyful ease.

Fields of giggles, rivers bright,
Swaying trees in sheer delight.
Sunshine beams with witty flair,
Every ray a laugh to share.

Priceless Punchlines

Words like bubbles, float and pop,
Each one's timing, always top.
Jokes whirl by in silly haste,
Charming winks, no time to waste.

Witty barbs, a playful jest,
Scatter laughter, that's the quest.
Every chuckle, a treasure found,
In this realm where joy abounds.

Stellar Sarcasm

Stars that wink, a cheeky glow,
Twinkling tales of high and low.
Shooting quips line the night sky,
Cosmic laughs that float and fly.

Planets spin with playful grace,
Grinning moons keep up the pace.
Reality wears a funny hat,
In this circus where we're at.

Mirthful Moonlit Valleys

In valleys where the jesters leap,
The moonlight winks, a secret to keep.
Dancing shadows play their tricks,
Unruly laughter, a joyous mix.

Silly tales are told at night,
Mirthful spirits taking flight.
The stars above join in the fun,
A cosmic party just begun.

The Pits of Playfulness

In playful pits where giggles thrive,
Silly antics come alive.
A tumble here, a slip in jest,
Laughter bubbles, truly blessed.

A whoopee cushion's hidden tune,
Echoes softly 'neath the moon.
Jokes unfold like flowers bloom,
Sparking joy, dispelling gloom.

Glee in the Shadows

In shadows long, the laughter grows,
Whispers of joy in playful throes.
Funny faces painted bright,
Underneath the soft starlight.

Echoes dance with a smirk and sway,
Mischief lurking, night turns gay.
Tickles shared among the crowd,
Joyful echoes, merry and loud.

Cosmic Chuckles

Across the vast and twinkling skies,
Planets giggle, stars reply.
Galaxies filled with glee and cheer,
Spinning jokes we long to hear.

A comet's tail, a playful tease,
Whirling laughter on the breeze.
In this dance of cosmic light,
Laughter echoes through the night.

Witty Impacts

In a world where laughter lands,
Jokes bounce like round rubber bands.
A slip, a trip, oh what a sight,
Giggles burst like stars at night.

Clumsy astronauts float in cheer,
Spinning tales, raising a beer.
Each stumble is a comic score,
As laughter echoes, evermore.

A ticklish comet flying by,
Winks and chuckles in the sky.
With punchlines scattered all around,
Joy erupts on comic ground.

So grab a joke as you take flight,
Through endless giggles, pure delight.
In every twist, in playful jest,
A universe of laughter's best.

Constellation Comedies

Stars twinkle with a cheeky grin,
Each one hides a joke within.
Planets dance in playful glee,
Shining bright for all to see.

Meteor showers of silly pranks,
Comics line up, form funny ranks.
Laughter echoes through the night,
As jokes collide in pure delight.

Galaxies filled with clever puns,
Whirling 'round like joyous runs.
In every corner, chuckles bloom,
As cosmic silliness finds room.

Join the jesters up in space,
With every punchline, find your place.
In this vast, comedic spree,
A tapestry of glee you'll see.

Jovial Jumpstarts

Bouncing beans in merry rows,
Each step brings laughter that overflows.
Hop and skip with giddy haste,
As we savor each funny taste.

Jokes are sprouted like wildflowers,
In the sunshine of funny hours.
Tickling tales from here to there,
Witty quips are in the air.

Jumpstarts of giggles spark the day,
Laughter lights a happy way.
In every twist and turn we find,
The joy that's bursting in our mind.

So leap into this comical ride,
With humor always by your side.
In every bounce, in every giggle,
The universe is full of wiggles.

The Asteroid of Amusement

An asteroid whirls, a chuckle flies,
With each spin, it sprinkles surprise.
Bouncing off the laughter beam,
Making even the grumpy beam.

Rolling laughter like a ball,
A joyride that won't let you fall.
Every twist is a punchline bright,
Creating smiles from pure delight.

Silly shapes in cosmic play,
Wonders of whimsy every day.
Comedic forces pull us near,
As we laugh away all our fear.

So ride the wave of playful fate,
On this rock, don't hesitate.
For in this orbit of pure fun,
We dance until the day is done.

Giggles from the Great Beyond

In the realm where laughs take flight,
Bubbles of humor dance in the night.
Witty whispers, echoes of glee,
A cosmic stage for all to see.

Floating in jest, a riotous swirl,
Funny faces in a whimsical whirl.
Stars chuckle bright with a playful gleam,
As laughter unfolds like a joyful dream.

Jokes like meteors, blazing and quick,
Comets with punchlines, a comic trick.
Each twinkle sparkles with mirthful delight,
A tapestry woven with humor's light.

Satire in Spherical Form

Round and round, the jokes take shape,
A merry-go-round of humor and hap.
From silly hats to quirky tunes,
The universe laughs under the moon.

Bouncing puns like bouncing balls,
Echoes of laughter fill the halls.
Each twist and turn, a witty jest,
In the spinning globe, we find our rest.

Parodies fly like balloons in the air,
Floating on whims, without a care.
Gravity's grip loosens on rhyme,
As laughter sings through the threads of time.

Joyful Eruptions

From the ground, laughter bursts forth,
Like bubbly magma, a comical worth.
Jokes erupt like fireworks bright,
Turning the mundane into delight.

Silly eruptions, a laughter spree,
Gags and giggles, set them free.
With every splash, humor unfolds,
Erupting tales that are pure gold.

A fountain of fun, heaven-sent,
Spraying cheer with each event.
The world shakes with chuckles and cheer,
As joyful bursts draw us near.

Comedic Caverns

In deep caverns, echoes of cheer,
Wit and whimsy linger near.
Stalactites dripping with snappy quips,
Laughter bounces off the craggy lips.

Within these walls, humor's embrace,
Jokes and jests have found their place.
Giggling shadows dance in the dark,
As comedy leaves its memorable mark.

Chucking stones, giggling all about,
A raucous chorus, no room for doubt.
In every nook, laughter takes a stand,
In comical caverns, we feel so grand.

Pranks in the Orbit

In outer space, they play their tricks,
A meteor dances, a comet flicks.
Aliens giggle, a cosmic jest,
With each new plan, they are truly blessed.

Invisible hats on the stars above,
They toss space pies with a laugh and shove.
Jokes float freely with no end in sight,
In the galactic theater, they laugh all night.

Black holes open like winks from the sky,
Swirling with mischief, oh me, oh my!
Asteroids tumble, a clumsy ballet,
Making the universe dance in a play.

Each planet chuckles, the sun snickers bright,
In a cosmic circus of pure delight.
From the rings of Saturn to Mars' own tune,
The laughter echoes, a whimsical boon.

Amusement in the Void

In the vast expanse where the silence reigns,
A gaggle of stars recounting their pains.
They tickle the moons, with a twinkle and tease,
As comets fly by with a whoosh and a wheeze.

Jovial giants with jovial sights,
Swap old jokes in the chill of the nights.
Nebulas giggle, all colors in play,
While whispers of laughter drift far away.

A quasar beams with a punchline unexpected,
And black holes swallow what's never detected.
The cosmos chuckles with each swirling rhyme,
Spinning tales of humor, defying all time.

The universe knows how to float with grace,
Dancing through darkness, a bright, happy place.
Galaxies join in the comic spree,
Creating a symphony of pure jubilee.

A Universe of Humor

Among the stars, where the laughter swells,
Martians tell tales with their quirky spells.
Planets in pairs, doing the macarena,
While asteroids roll, a cosmic ballerina.

The space-time continuum bends with the joke,
As meteors burst into giggles and smoke.
Light years fly by with a punchline so fine,
Galactic chuckles, a universal sign.

Shooting stars wishing for laughter to last,
As the cosmos giggles, a blast from the past.
Wormholes open like doors to delight,
Inviting the void to join in the light.

So gather your friends in this comedic spree,
In the vastness of space, let's all dance free.
For in this grand tale where humor resides,
Every laugh echoes, in the galaxy, it glides.

The Jovial Void

In the dark, where laughter swirls,
A circus of stars does twirl.
Punch lines dance in cosmic play,
Grins ignite the Milky Way.

Asteroids in jest collide,
With silly masks, they try to hide.
Giggles escape from planetary zones,
Making jokes with funny tones.

Nebulae burst into bright hues,
Witty quips in vibrant views.
Each puff of dust, a jest untold,
Sparkling laughter, pure and bold.

In this vast and wondrous space,
Joyful antics find their place.
While comets race and planets spin,
The universe wears a cheeky grin.

Satellite Chuckles

Around the world, they zoom and glide,
Carrying laughter far and wide.
With antennae catching giggly sounds,
They beam joy where laughter bounds.

Each spin brings forth a punchy tale,
Satellites dance in cosmic hail.
Jokes orbit tight in comic spins,
As starlight twinkles, a grin begins.

From the moon, wisecracks take flight,
In this vast comedic night.
Jovial beams from space unwind,
In orbits where laughter is designed.

With every twist and playful jest,
They tickle time, they never rest.
In this show of bright delight,
Cosmic comedy shines so bright.

Gales of Glee

Breezes tickle cosmic ears,
As humor floats amidst the spheres.
Whispers of joy in every swirl,
A universe where laughter twirls.

From meteor showers, giggles rain,
Making light of cosmic pain.
Witty winks from shooting stars,
Jocularity from Venus to Mars.

The galaxies hum a merry tune,
As quips fly high, from sun to moon.
In every gust, a punchline gleams,
Building dreams from gales of beams.

Through the void, a cheerful rush,
Inside this laughter-fueled hush.
Every whirl and playful breeze,
Crafts a universe of ease.

Celestial Comedy Tales

Once upon a starlit space,
A funny tale of cosmic grace.
Where planets wear their best charade,
And comets tease in grand parade.

With every twist, a silly fate,
Astronauts giggle at every plate.
As spaced-out jokes around them soar,
The cosmos laughs forevermore.

Saturn's rings in jolly spins,
A ringmaster where laughter wins.
Galaxies twinkle in delight,
As joke-laden echoes fill the night.

In the fabric of the cosmic yarn,
Witticisms sparkle, bright as dawn.
With every turn, a story blooms,
In swirling stars, joy finds its rooms.

Laughter's Landscape

In a field where giggles grow,
Tickles sprout in a playful row.
Jokes dangle from the trees up high,
As punchlines fall like birds that fly.

The daisies dance in silly breeze,
As humor wafts with playful ease.
Beneath the sun, we laugh aloud,
In this bright spot, a jester's crowd.

A river flows with wit so bright,
It sparkles under the moonlight.
We dip our toes in laugh-filled streams,
And drift away on laughter's dreams.

Orbit of Amusement

In circles round, we spin and twirl,
With every giggle, we unfurl.
A cosmic dance of jest and cheer,
As laughter rockets far and near.

The satellites of jokes do soar,
Around our heads, they play and roar.
Comets made of chuckles glide,
Through galaxies where puns reside.

Asteroids of mirth whiz by,
Brightening the darkened sky.
In this vast space of joy so free,
We orbit on in harmony.

Playful Pockmarks

In every dent, a story waits,
Where laughter dances, and joy creates.
Each little dip, a tale unfolds,
Of silly moments, brave and bold.

The nooks and crannies, treasures found,
In playful pockmarks, joy is bound.
Echoes of laughter, soft and sweet,
In these small spots where friends do meet.

A patch of green is laughter's seat,
With games of tag, oh what a treat!
The shadows hide a playful grin,
As we dive deep and let love win.

Jovial Eruptions

From smiles that burst like joyful flames,
Eruptions spark with fun-filled names.
Laughter spilling in cascades bright,
A fountain of glee in the busy night.

Giggles bubble and tickles rise,
Erupting joy that never lies.
The earth shakes with a laugh so true,
In this raucous fun, we renew.

With every boom, the tensions flee,
A celebration of pure glee.
In this jovial space, we play and prance,
As laughter's rhythm gives us a chance.

Cosmic Quips

In the void where laughter's born,
Stars twinkle like jokes, all adorned.
Comets zoom with punchlines bright,
Galaxy giggles ignite the night.

Planets spin with playful tease,
Orbiting dreams that aim to please.
Asteroids chuckle, bumping around,
In this vast playground, joy's profound.

Nebulas swirl in colors bold,
Each hue a jest, a tale retold.
Supernovae burst with a shout,
Creating hilarity all about.

So look to the skies, don't just gaze,
The cosmos dances in humorous ways.
For every black hole, a prankster's grin,
In the vast universe, joy's just a spin.

Spherical Serenades

Round like the world, the jesters sing,
Bouncing quips that joy can bring.
Each note a laugh, each chord a cheer,
Melodies of mirth ring loud and clear.

Planets play with light and sound,
In their orbits, smiles abound.
Gravity's pull, a ticklish bind,
As stars align to see what's kind.

Spherical tales of whimsy weave,
Lunar laughs that never leave.
In the embrace of night's warm glow,
A symphony of giggles flows.

So join the dance of the cosmic tune,
Under the watch of the chuckling moon.
With each twirl, a jocular delight,
In the universe, everything's bright.

Humor in the Abyss

In the depths where shadows play,
Whispers of jest make darkness sway.
Giggles echo through the yonder,
In the void where we ponder.

Jokes float like bubbles in the deep,
Tickling souls, their secrets keep.
Monsters laugh, no fright in sight,
Their humor glows, a strange light.

Drifting down with a gentle grace,
Finding smiles in a solemn space.
Each ripple's a laugh, a twist of fate,
In this abyss, we celebrate.

So plunge into laughter, take the dive,
In the dark, humor's alive.
For beneath the waves, we find our cheer,
Eclipsing gloom with joy sincere.

Silvery Snickers

Beneath the moon's soft, silver glow,
Whispered giggles start to flow.
Starlit winks from above so high,
As the night chuckles, oh my, oh my!

Clouds drift in like fluffy jesters,
Mimicking life's oddball testers.
Each twinkling star a wry remark,
Illuminating joy in the dark.

Comets laugh as they dart and gleam,
Painting the sky with a giddy dream.
In this celestial theater's show,
Every wink tells us to let go.

So find the fun in each tickling breath,
Embrace the jokes, dance with depth.
For life is a stage, so play your part,
In the cosmos above, joy's the heart.

Laughter's Landing

In a place where giggles bloom,
And jokes light up the room,
Clowns juggle stars with grace,
Each chuckle finds its place.

Balloons float, painted bright,
Whispers of joy take flight,
Tickles dance upon the breeze,
As smiles spring forth with ease.

Laughter bubbles, spills like wine,
Each punchline a secret sign,
Mirthful echoes filled with cheer,
In this land, we lose our fear.

So join the fun, forget the norm,
Let silliness be the form,
At Laughter's Landing, every heart
Finds joy in its curious art.

Humor's Hidden Depths

Dive into the depths below,
Where giggles hide and wisecracks flow,
Beneath the surface, jesters play,
Crafting laughter in their way.

Mysteries wrapped in comic cheer,
Echoing jokes for all to hear,
With every splash, a grin appears,
As humor conquers all our fears.

Witty lines like fish that leap,
In tangled nets, their secrets keep,
Explore the depths where laughter swims,
In pools of joy, the spirit brims.

So let us delve, embrace the fun,
Where punchlines dance and we become,
Adventurers in mirthful fates,
In Humor's depths, joy awaits.

Punchlines in the Past

Echoes of laughter from days gone by,
Stories told with a twinkle-eye,
Each punchline thrown, a memory cast,
A tapestry of humor vast.

Time travelers in jest we roam,
Gathering smiles to take us home,
The past unfolds in giggles sweet,
As old jokes become our treat.

From vaudeville to silent glee,
Every era, a new decree,
We laugh at blunders, slip on tricks,
A time machine made of comic picks.

So join us now, in yesteryear,
Where laughter echoes, crystal clear,
Punchlines linger, never fade,
In the past, our joy is made.

Whimsical Wonders of the Void

In a cosmic dance of the absurd,
Where silence speaks, and stars are stirred,
Galaxies twinkle with laughter's grace,
In the void, we find our place.

Jokes hang like comets in the night,
Each one a spark of pure delight,
With every chuckle, we float and swirl,
In whimsical wonders, dreams unfurl.

Aliens laugh in quirky tongues,
As gravity pulls on silly songs,
Floating through this cosmic jest,
We find humor at its best.

So take a leap into the bizarre,
Dance with the echoes of a shooting star,
In the void where whims abound,
Laughter's magic knows no ground.

Gravitational Gags

A bouncy ball on a sunny day,
It rolls away in a merry play.
The cat chases it, leaps with a laugh,
In a world where gravity takes a photograph.

A banana peel on a crowded street,
Someone slips, oh what a feat!
Laughter erupts like a mighty storm,
In a universe where falls keep warm.

Each snicker zooms like a shooting star,
Twirling through space, never too far.
Joy spirals round in a cosmic dance,
Under the spotlight, give giggles a chance.

Stars wink down at the playful glee,
As hiccups and snorts set humor free.
In the vastness, silliness prevails,
Through the void of laughter, fun never fails.

The Joyful Descent

Sliding down laughter's slippery slope,
Tickling toes with humor and hope.
A jester's leap into a pie,
With whipped cream clouds floating by.

Chasing the echoes of silly sounds,
Where giggles bounce and joy abounds.
A tumble here, a pratfall there,
In this joyful descent, none can despair.

Each dizzy spin brings smiles anew,
Wit dances gracefully, a lively crew.
Laughter erupts, a contagious cheer,
As friends gather 'round, the fun is clear.

Through the whirl and the whirl, we collide,
In this cosmic carnival, take a ride.
Every hearty laugh, a shooting star,
Guiding us home from wherever we are.

Nebulae of Nonsense

In a galaxy of giggles, clouds form,
Nonsense spins in a riotous storm.
A ticklish comet zooms past our sight,
Flinging jokes in the heart of the night.

Whirling through absurdity's bright hues,
Fragments of humor bursting like jewels.
Chasing the echoes of a playful muse,
Where laughter erupts and joy flees the blues.

Jars of pickles wearing funny hats,
Spacecats purring while lying on mats.
Jokes collide like stars in the dark,
Creating a universe filled with spark.

With each burst of laughter, planets align,
Creating a rhythm, a cosmic rhyme.
In the nebulae, we find our bliss,
Lost in a melody of giggles and twists.

Whirlwind of Wit

In a storm of humor, wit takes flight,
Spinning and twirling in sheer delight.
The punchlines flutter, like leaves in a breeze,
Tickling our senses, the mind's sweet tease.

Round and round, the laughter swirls,
With clever jabs and playful pearls.
Weaving tales of the day's best flops,
In this tempest, the silliness never stops.

A juggler fumbles, and oranges rain,
Crisp bursts of laughter mixed with joy and pain.
Each silly moment, a vibrant spark,
Creating a canvas from light and dark.

So join the dance, let the jokes unfurl,
In the whirlwind of wit, let laughter swirl.
Spin with abandon, don't hold it tight,
In this glorious chaos, everything feels right.

Moonlit Merriment

Under the stars, laughter spills,
Jovial jests, like cosmic thrills.
Bouncing moonbeams, silly pranks,
Galactic giggles fill the ranks.

Whirling in space, the fun takes flight,
Comets dance, oh what a sight!
In this bright night, all troubles cease,
Each chuckle ignites a new release.

Gravity can't hold back our cheer,
Starry clowns drawing ever near.
With meteor jokes and cosmic glee,
A universe painted in hilarity.

So gather round, in this lofty realm,
Where joy is king, and laughter's helm.
The milky way glimmers with playful spark,
In this night sky, we leave our mark.

Celestial Capers

Shooting stars with wit so sharp,
They light the way, a laugh-filled park.
Planetary pranks in swirling play,
Universes grin, come join the fray.

Galaxies twirl in joyful spins,
Every comet wears a silly grin.
Asteroids tumble with a flip,
In this wild ride, we take a trip.

Nebulae burst with jokes and jives,
In outer space, fun truly thrives.
Solar flares wink, teasingly bright,
In this vast expanse, hearts feel light.

So lift your voice, let laughter soar,
Join the dance by the cosmic door.
In the brilliance of starlit trails,
The joy of the universe never fails.

Cosmic Caves of Humor

In caverns deep where stardust swirls,
Funny echoes dance, laughter twirls.
Galactic glee in every nook,
Where jovial spirits play the book.

Comets whisper hilarious tales,
In this cavern, laughter sails.
Echoing shapes make mischief bright,
In the shadows, we feel the light.

Planets peek in, curious to see,
What hilarious antics there could be.
Jokes ignite like shooting stars,
In this cosmic playground, joy is ours.

So join the fun in this sparkling sphere,
As laughter rolls in whispers clear.
With cosmic caves full of delightful cheer,
Every chuckle takes away the fear.

Echoed Euphoria

In the silence of space, laughter rings,
Joyful echoes of cosmic flings.
Starry gaffes and silly fables,
In this vast void, we build our tables.

With twinkling stars as our backdrop,
Every joke lifts us, we just can't stop.
Galactic chuckles bounce off the moon,
In the great expanse, we find our tune.

Black holes hide the punchlines bright,
Swallowing woes in the endless night.
With comets as props and quirks in tow,
In this euphoria, let laughter flow.

So gather, friends, in this boundless embrace,
Where echoes of joy fill every space.
In the cosmos, our spirits soar,
In the giggles shared, we find much more.

Echoes from the Unseen

In shadows deep where giggles play,
The unseen worlds create their sway.
With whispers soft that tickle the night,
Echoes bounce with pure delight.

A cosmic dance of jest and cheer,
Planetary chaos drawing near.
The stars, they wink, applauding the scene,
As laughter spills from where we've been.

Each crater holds a joke or two,
In lunar lands where smiles grew.
They spill their secrets, gleefully shared,
In the vastness, joy is declared.

So join the jesters, take your flight,
Under the moon's embrace so bright.
In unseen realms, we'll laugh and spin,
For humor lives where dreams begin.

Lunar Laughter

A silver orb, so round and bright,
Hides silly tales in the pale moonlight.
Each crater wears a cheeky grin,
Inviting all to dive right in.

Through patches soft where shadows dart,
The moonlight sows a playful heart.
With giggles tossed to cosmic winds,
The universe invites our whims.

Frolicking foxes, dancing bears,
In galaxies beyond our cares.
The moon's soft glow, a comic muse,
In lunar realms there's no excuse.

Let's raise a toast to lunar cheer,
Where space and laughter blend so near.
A cosmic giggle, a shared delight,
In every moonbeam, laughter's light.

Echoes of Jest

In playful orbits, laughter spins,
Cascading down where humor begins.
A waltz of stars, a jovial blend,
With echoes of jest that never end.

Each crater holds a story rare,
Of cosmic pranks spun through the air.
With chuckles bursting from afar,
The night sky zings a wink and spar.

In muted tones, the whispers flow,
From shimmering worlds where giggles grow.
The cosmic stage, a vibrant scene,
A funny ballet, the unseen queen.

So let your spirit dance and twirl,
With those who laugh and hearts that whirl.
In every echo, joy insists,
And every night, the jest persists.

The Moon's Chuckle

Above the world, so high and wide,
The moon holds joys we cannot hide.
In winks and nudges, softly bright,
It shares its humor in the night.

Beneath the gaze of craters' smiles,
We wander through the cosmic miles.
With every twinkle, quips abound,
In lunar lands, pure joy is found.

The stars are jesters, wild and free,
Their playful glances, a comedy.
In laughter's realm, our spirits soar,
As moonbeams light the joyful floor.

So join the dance and spin around,
In laughter's grasp, we all are bound.
In every chuckle, magic swirls,
For humor's charm is out of this world.

The Mirthful Moon

In the night sky, a giggle so bright,
Lunar faces jest, a comical sight.
Stars join in laughter, swirls of delight,
With every wink, they tickle the night.

Bouncing across craters, glee takes flight,
Casting jokes in the shadows of light.
Each crater a scene, a stand-up rite,
The moon cracks up, oh what a height!

With playful giggles, the cosmos spins,
Galaxies chuckle, where humor begins.
In the glow of joy, the universe grins,
A cosmic carnival, where love always wins.

So when you gaze up, take a moment to see,
The moon's laughter, wild and free.
Join in the fun, let your spirit be,
A part of the jests, in this grand jamboree.

Celestial Comedy Clubs

In the vast expanse, a stage is set,
Where meteors dance, no sign of regret.
Comedians twinkle, each joke a bet,
A cosmic space where laughter is met.

Galactic punchlines, swirling in light,
Planets are patrons, laughing all night.
Asteroids clap, what a curious sight,
As comets crack jokes, igniting delight.

Stars take the mic, in playful spree,
Each orb shares a tale, a funny decree.
In this cosmic club, all are carefree,
Bathed in the warmth of shared glee.

So raise a toast, to the skies above,
In this celestial scene, you'll find love.
Laughter echoes, like a soft glove,
In the universe's heart, we all fit like a dove.

Comets of Cheer

Zooming through space, a vibrant trail,
Comets bring smiles, a joke on the sail.
With laughter in tow, they set off to wail,
A whimsical journey, where chuckles prevail.

Whirling around planets, a jig they will do,
Bright streaks of joy, a comedic review.
Each flash a punchline, fresh as the dew,
In the cosmic audience, laughter is true.

Twinkling with mirth, they dance and they glide,
Joyous navigation, in laughter they pride.
With bright tails of humor, they joyously ride,
In this universe grand, love is our guide.

So look to the sky when you're feeling down,
Let comets of cheer wear a bright, funny crown.
In their light-filled wake, let joy be renowned,
Together we'll smile, in laughter we drown.

Laughter's Lightyear

A journey of joy, at light-speed we soar,
Chasing the giggles from galaxy's core.
With every tickle, we want to explore,
The universe chuckles, what's not to adore?

Time travelers laughing, in joyous embrace,
Every moment we share, a fun-filled space.
With laughter as fuel, we quicken our pace,
Past comets and stars, in a bright, funny race.

Each corner we turn, there's humor to find,
In places unseen, where funny's entwined.
The cosmos rejoices, laughter's designed,
A lightyear of giggles, all hearts unconfined.

So strap in your seat and prepare for the ride,
Through laughter's expanse, let joy be your guide.
In this stellar dance, let the humor reside,
As we journey together, laughter's true tide.

The Humor that Bubbles

Laughter rises like a fizzy drink,
With every pop, we grin and wink.
Bubbles dance in silly cheer,
As jokes take flight, oh my, oh dear!

A rubber chicken in the sky,
It flaps its wings, oh how we cry!
The punchline lands, a slip and slide,
In this funny world, we take a ride.

Faces painted, silly hats,
A parade of laughter, where joy is at.
Tickles in the air, can you feel?
Wiggling toes, a grand reveal!

So let the giggles bubble high,
With every chuckle, reach the sky.
In this humor, we delight,
Together we soar, oh what a sight!

Celestial Jests

Stars collide in comic flair,
Galaxies giggle in midair.
Planets roll with laughter bright,
In the cosmos, our hearts take flight.

Comets zoom with a honk and cheer,
Their tails a joke we all can hear.
Asteroids bob, a dance so bold,
In the universe, fun unfolds.

A moonbeam chuckles, soft and light,
Casting shadows that twist in delight.
We twirl in orbits, never still,
In this vast space, it's laughter we fill.

So let the stellar jokes abound,
In every corner, joy is found.
Galactic giggles, shining glare,
Together we soar, without a care!

Dark Pits of Delight

In shadowy nooks, we find our glee,
With eerie echoes and ghoulish spree.
Monsters boast of threats so dire,
But their clumsy steps inspire a choir.

Witches cackle on crooked brooms,
While goblins dance in endless rooms.
In the spooky dark, joy takes its place,
As we trip on laughter, a right silly race.

Haunted halls with cats that meow,
They tease and play, oh, take a bow!
Boo! they shout, with playful fright,
In this odd realm, we scream with delight.

So wander deep in these pits of cheer,
Where every shadow whispers near.
Among the frights, we find our way,
In darkened corners, laughter's play!

Astral Amusement

In the cosmos where giggles sprout,
Cosmic clowns twirl about.
Nebulas flash with colorful glee,
As stardust dances, wild and free.

The sun grins wide, a happy ray,
Spinning tales of humor play.
Eclipses make the light play tricks,
In this expanse, joy kicks!

Saturn's rings jingle with delight,
Jovial jesters spin through the night.
In this astral sphere, we fall and laugh,
Chasing our dreams in a cosmic path.

So gaze at the stars and take your flight,
With laughter guiding, all feels right.
In the universe vast, joy's our theme,
Together we float, living the dream!

Laughter's Terrain

In valleys where chuckles bloom,
Jesters dance, dispelling gloom.
With every slip and playful trip,
Joy spills out in a wild quip.

Bubbles pop, and soda sprays,
Silly hats for silly days.
Each snicker wraps the world in glee,
Oh, what fun this place can be!

Where silly songs fill up the air,
And tickles lurk with cheeky flair.
A tumble here, a pratfall there,
Laughter echoes everywhere.

In laughter's land, we lose our woe,
With friends around, the joy will flow.
A carnival of hearts aligned,
In every giggle, we unwind.

Gala of Giggles

The evening glows with bright delight,
As punchlines soar like stars at night.
Each joke spins in a merry dance,
Inviting every soul to prance.

With playful pies and cream-filled dreams,
In every chuckle, magic beams.
The lights all twinkle, laughter rings,
A chorus joyful, oh how it sings!

Jokers jive with joyful flair,
While dancers trip without a care.
A funny hat parade goes wide,
As giggles grow, there's nowhere to hide.

In this gala, troubles fade,
As gags and glee serenely invade.
Whimsical whims take center stage,
In this festooned, hilarious cage.

Silent Craters, Loud Laughs

In quiet nooks where whispers thrive,
A ticklish breeze gives jokes a drive.
Unexpected slips and merry falls,
In silence, laughter sweetly calls.

Echoes bounce in the stillness here,
Every chuckle brings us cheer.
Loud laughs spring like a sudden rain,
Dancing hearts with joyous strain.

A funny face and wiggly dance,
In whispered worlds, we take a chance.
With each heartbeat, the laughter grows,
In silent craters, joy just flows.

Loud laughs burst, a playful storm,
In every corner, hearts are warm.
Where humor hides and will resound,
The silent craters, joy is found.

Cosmic Jest Fest

Across the stars where giggles shine,
The universe hums with humor divine.
Galaxies swirl in a playful spin,
As cosmic jesters invite us in.

Comets swerve with a punchline's flair,
While space-time bends with jokes to share.
A little moon with a winking gaze,
Reminds us all to laugh and praise.

In this festival of stars and dreams,
Every chuckle gleams and beams.
Strange planets wobble with joyous sound,
As humor in the cosmos is found.

With every tickle from a shooting star,
We find the giggles, near and far.
In this vast expanse, we find the jest,
In cosmic joy, we are truly blessed.

Jests from the Stars

In the sky where laughter glows,
Planets spin in silly shows.
Comets chase with goofy grins,
While shooting stars play peekaboo spins.

Galaxies burst in fits of cheer,
Whispering jokes from far and near.
Nebulas twirl in swirling glee,
A cosmic dance of playful spree.

Astronauts giggle in weightless trails,
Witty quips float like feathered sails.
With each bounce across the void,
They share the jest, laughter unalloyed.

In orbits wild, the humor plays,
Making light of the dark maze.
Stellar wisdom, winks, and grins,
In this vastness, the fun begins.

Asteroid Antics

Rolling rocks with cheeky flair,
Bouncing through the cosmic air.
They crack jokes and play all day,
In the asteroid belt, come what may.

Comets collide with laughter loud,
Each mishap drawing a merry crowd.
One trips over while chasing light,
Stumbling softly in pure delight.

They juggle moons, they dance on rays,
Creating chaos in funny ways.
With every twist, a chuckle shared,
In this space, no need for baired.

Asteroids gather under starlit beams,
Telling tales woven with dreams.
The universe chuckles at their games,
As laughter echoes through the names.

Jovial Chasms

Deep in the valleys of lunar lands,
Echoes of giggles drift in strands.
Playing tricks with gravity's charm,
The cliffs smile back, safe from harm.

Shadows stretch to dance and sway,
Banter rings out in bright array.
Each crevice holds a silly sight,
As moonbeams laugh, embracing the night.

Laughter bubbles from every crack,
Stars bounce back with no lack of knack.
In these depths, the jesters roam,
Finding joy far away from home.

The moons above join in the fun,
Winking bright like rays of sun.
In jovial chasms, the joy cascades,
A universe where laughter pervades.

Bubbles of Banter

Floating softly through cosmic sea,
Bubbles burst with banter free.
Each pop sends ripples of delight,
Illuminating the starry night.

Silly voices in gentle sways,
Echoing through the starry rays.
With every spark, a giggle's found,
As laughter dances all around.

Colors splash as jokes collide,
Each bubble drawing smiles wide.
From star to star, the laughter flies,
In this vastness, joy never dies.

So drift along the starlit skies,
Letting go of frowns and sighs.
In bubbles of banter, we stay afloat,
Sailing on laughter, like a joyful boat.

Cosmic Matinee

In the theater of space, stars play their part,
Galactic giggles echo, a celestial art.
Planets spin jigs, comets dance free,
A wondrous show, just wait and see!

Asteroids humorously tumble and roll,
While meteors sparkle, igniting the soul.
With every blink, a joke is told,
This cosmic circus, a sight to behold!

Laughter in orbits, we float in delight,
Each twinkling light, a punchline in flight.
Nebulae chuckle in colors so bright,
Spinning through decades, a ripple of night.

So grab your popcorn, let's watch the stars,
Across the vast stages with laughter from Mars.
The universe loves to tickle and tease,
In this cosmic matinee, we're bound to please!

Echoes of Elation

In the void, joy bounces, a vibrant sound,
As laughter rings out from planets around.
With each cosmic joke, the silence breaks,
Echoes of elation, the universe quakes.

Galaxies spin, with chuckles that soar,
Whispers of joy from a million stars more.
Wormholes connect us, with giggles so grand,
In this dance of delight, we all understand.

Every quasar's blink is a wink in disguise,
Brightening our nights with spectacular skies.
Through cosmic confetti, we twirl with glee,
In echoes of laughter, forever we're free.

So, toast to the heavens, raise your glass high,
As stardust and humor take flight through the sky.
In this musing of mirth, we drift and glide,
Echoes of elation forever our guide.

Galaxies of Guffaws

In the spiral embrace of a laughing galore,
Stars burst in laughter, creating folklore.
Each twinkle a tease, each cluster a "Why?"
As comets streak past with a wink to the sky.

Supernovae explode with vibrant delight,
While black holes churn jokes, out of sight.
The cosmos a stage, where hilarity reigns,
Galaxies swirling, in whimsical trains.

Gravity pulls us, yet we float on air,
With every giggle woven, a cosmic affair.
In this universe full of whimsical threads,
Each planet a puppet, with laughter it spreads.

So gather your friends, raise a toast to the fun,
For in this grand show, we're all under one sun.
With galaxies booming, their laughter won't cease,
In the vastness of space, we all find our peace.

A Milky Way of Mirth

Drifting through ribbons of creamy delight,
We find joy in spaces, both cosmic and bright.
Stars play peek-a-boo, behind clouds of fluff,
In this Milky Way of mirth, ample enough.

Comets with candy trails dash past our view,
Spreading sweetness and giggles in their wake too.
With each galactic giggle, we spin and we sway,
In the dance of the heavens, we frolic and play.

Shooting stars wink, igniting our dreams,
While celestial bodies scheme in bright beams.
The universe chuckles, a grand cosmic joke,
In this swirling star cookies, laughter's the smoke.

So as we sail through this humorous sea,
Finding joy in stardust, you and me.
With a wink from the cosmos, we're never alone,
In this Milky Way of mirth, joy is our home.

Chuckles in the Cosmic Dust

In the vacuum where laughs take flight,
Stars giggle and twinkle through the night.
Asteroids tumble, a slapstick scene,
With comets tailing like a clownish dream.

Planets wobble in a dizzy dance,
Gravity pulls them, but still they prance.
A Jupiter jester with rings so wide,
Spinning tales, where humor can't hide.

Lunar legends light up the skies,
With meteoric mimes in disguise.
Through nebulae, we chase the jest,
Finding laughter in the cosmic quest.

So float on laughter, join the fun,
In this universe of puns that stun.
A celestial circus, wild and free,
Where every moment is comedy's decree.

The Gagged Galaxies

In a swirl of stars, the giggles rise,
Bright nebulae hide behind their sighs.
Amidst the chaos, a joke takes flight,
Comedic wonders in the endless night.

Black holes chuckle with a cosmic pull,
Swallowing puns, their mouths a full.
While shooting stars race for the punchline,
Fumbling and tumbling, oh how divine!

Galactic gags spread light years wide,
Jovial jesters on a cosmic ride.
With laughter echoing through the void,
Each star a punchline, never destroyed.

So when you gaze at the heavens aglow,
Remember the humor in the cosmic show.
For in the galaxies, where mirth collides,
Lies a universe where laughter abides.

Jovial Gorges

In valleys where laughter echoes and peals,
Over cliffs where the starlight squeals.
Echoing giggles in the canyon deep,
Whispers of joy that never sleep.

Comedic craters in the surface they make,
With each little bump, a shake and a quake.
Through jovial gorges, the spirits soar,
Beneath the horizon, forever encore.

Sunlight cascades across the floor,
Tickling the rocks, they giggle and roar.
With each twist and turn, a jest awaits,
In the playful depths where humor creates.

So wander these paths of fun and mirth,
Where laughter resounds, and joy gives birth.
In joyful gorges, we find delight,
Turning woes into chuckles all night.

Grins from the Great Expanse

Across the vastness where starlight beams,
Laughter ripples like gurgling streams.
The universe giggles, a sight to behold,
With comets telling tales of old.

Hulks of planets burst forth in glee,
As echoes bounce off the cosmic sea.
Silly shadows dance in the void,
With every twirl, the silence destroyed.

Skyward we drift on a wave of jest,
Finding joy in the vastness, our quest.
From supernovae that shine so bright,
To countless smiles from day to night.

So let us celebrate this space so grand,
Where humor and wonder hold each other's hand.
In the great expanse, let laughter take flight,
A cosmic chorus, a pure delight.

The Comedic Collision

In space, a clumsy dance,
With stars that stumble and prance,
A meteor's silly swoon,
Makes laughter echo like a tune.

Planets wobble, trying to spin,
As cosmic jokers throw a grin,
Asteroids wearing goofy hats,
Dance with bright and bouncing bats.

Supernova bursts in glee,
Shooting jokes like comedy,
Galaxies swirling with delight,
While moons chuckle through the night.

So let the universe be your stage,
Where humor shines and breaks the cage,
With each collision, tumble, and twirl,
The cosmos laughs, a vibrant whirl.

Cosmic Laughter Lines

In the void where jokes are born,
Starry giggles grace the morn,
Nebulae painted with delight,
Tickling comets in their flight.

Across the void, a supernova,
Explodes with humor, oh-so clever,
Sending ripples, laughter spread,
Echoing tales of fun ahead.

Quantum quips in cosmic jest,
Where asteroids play comedic chess,
And black holes boast of their size,
While giving sly, mischievous eyes.

Let humor guide this astral spree,
Where every punchline's wild and free,
In the universe's playful mime,
Laughter transcends the bounds of time.

Giggling Obsidian

Amidst the dark, a chuckle glows,
A tale where silly humor flows,
Obsidian rocks with laughter bright,
Bouncing joy in endless night.

Lava lamps of cosmic cheer,
Glow with jokes for all to hear,
Giggles spewing from volcanic cracks,
As joy erupts and never slacks.

Flickering stardust sparkles wide,
With every giggle, they collide,
And black surfaces crack with glee,
In this cosmic comedy spree.

So join the mirth in dark abyss,
Where laughs and joy coexist,
In every crater, every seam,
Laughter's pulse, a radiant dream.

Quasar Quips

In the mask of night, a radiant jest,
Quasars shine, they're truly blessed,
Their luminous beams bring smiles and wit,
Casting shadows where humor is lit.

Joking light-years, sending their beams,
Weaving through space like playful dreams,
With every quip that races by,
Mirth echoes in the sapphire sky.

Galactic giggles, sure to amaze,
Astrophysics lost in a playful haze,
As cosmic forces nudge and tease,
Creating a laughter-bound breeze.

So here's to quips that stretch and bend,
A humor journey that has no end,
In every twinkle, every spark,
Cosmic laughter lights the dark.

Lunar Laughter

In the moonlit glow, a jest takes flight,
With craters that giggle under the night.
Stars twinkle in rhythm, a cosmic play,
As shadows dance in a whimsical sway.

Rabbits in space wear hats of cheese,
Tickling the orbs with a light-hearted tease.
Gravity chuckles, pulls you near,
In this orbit of joy, laughter is clear.

Giggling rocks and swirling dust,
Poking fun at the cosmic trust.
When the sun yawns wide, jokes unfold,
In the universe's arms, we're never too old.

So let's take a ride on this merry spree,
Where humor paints the sky with glee.
With each soft bounce and playful tag,
We find our joy in the lunar rag.

Echoes of Hilarity

In the depths where laughter breathes,
Echoes bubble, teasing leaves.
Giggles roll on the surface bright,
Rolling like marbles under the light.

Voices of jest stretch far and wide,
Bouncing off valleys, they skip and slide.
A chorus of chuckles play the game,
Leaving no heart untouched, no one the same.

Underneath the playful skies,
Even the silence wears a disguise.
In the realm of joy, it's never absurd,
For every whisper is a joke unheard.

So let's dance on beams of light and cheer,
Finding laughter's joy, we always stay near.
With echoes that tickle, we join the fun,
Each chuckle we share marks a moment won.

Jokes from the Abyss

In the deep where shadows sigh,
Lies a treasure of humor, oh my!
With grinning faces in the gloom,
They tickle the void, dispelling doom.

Beneath the surface, punchlines swell,
As creatures in darkness weave their spell.
Slipping and sliding in playful cheer,
Every echo bursts, far and near.

What lies down here? Just a laugh, my friend,
As fables twist and always bend.
With riddles and giggles swirling around,
The abyss holds joy, quietly profound.

So join in this revelry from the deep,
Where humor awakens what we keep.
With each hearty laugh, we boldly persist,
In this ocean of joy, we cannot resist.

Smile Shaped Hollows

Nestled within are hollows bright,
Each shaped with laughter, pure delight.
Where beams of joy flicker and bounce,
In these spaces, giggles pounce.

With every turn of the whimsical grin,
The world inside begins to spin.
Echoes of chuckles rise and twirl,
In this joyful nook, bright dreams unfurl.

Jokes woven tight in laughter's weave,
Drawing all who dare believe.
Discovering moments, hard to miss,
In these smiles, we find our bliss.

So come share the glow in these gentle bays,
Where humor lingers and plays.
Each smile shaped hollow tells a tale,
In unity of laughter, we shall prevail.

www.ingramcontent.com/pod-product-compliance
Lightning Source LLC
Chambersburg PA
CBHW051642160426
43209CB00004B/756